Saving badgers

Liz Lewis

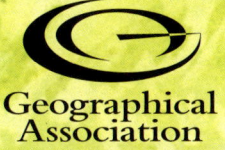

Geographical Association

A badger had come out to eat his food, from his home in a sett in Wayside Wood.

There was the badger sett, under a tree, but coloured tape showed where a new road would be.

'That's terrible!' Barnaby said with a frown. 'When he crosses the road badger might get knocked down.'

The children worked hard and they wrote a report.
People signed a petition to give them support.

A map of the trail was made and it showed, a plan for a tunnel built under the road.

They wrote to the Council and said in their letter, 'For the badgers a tunnel would be so much better!'

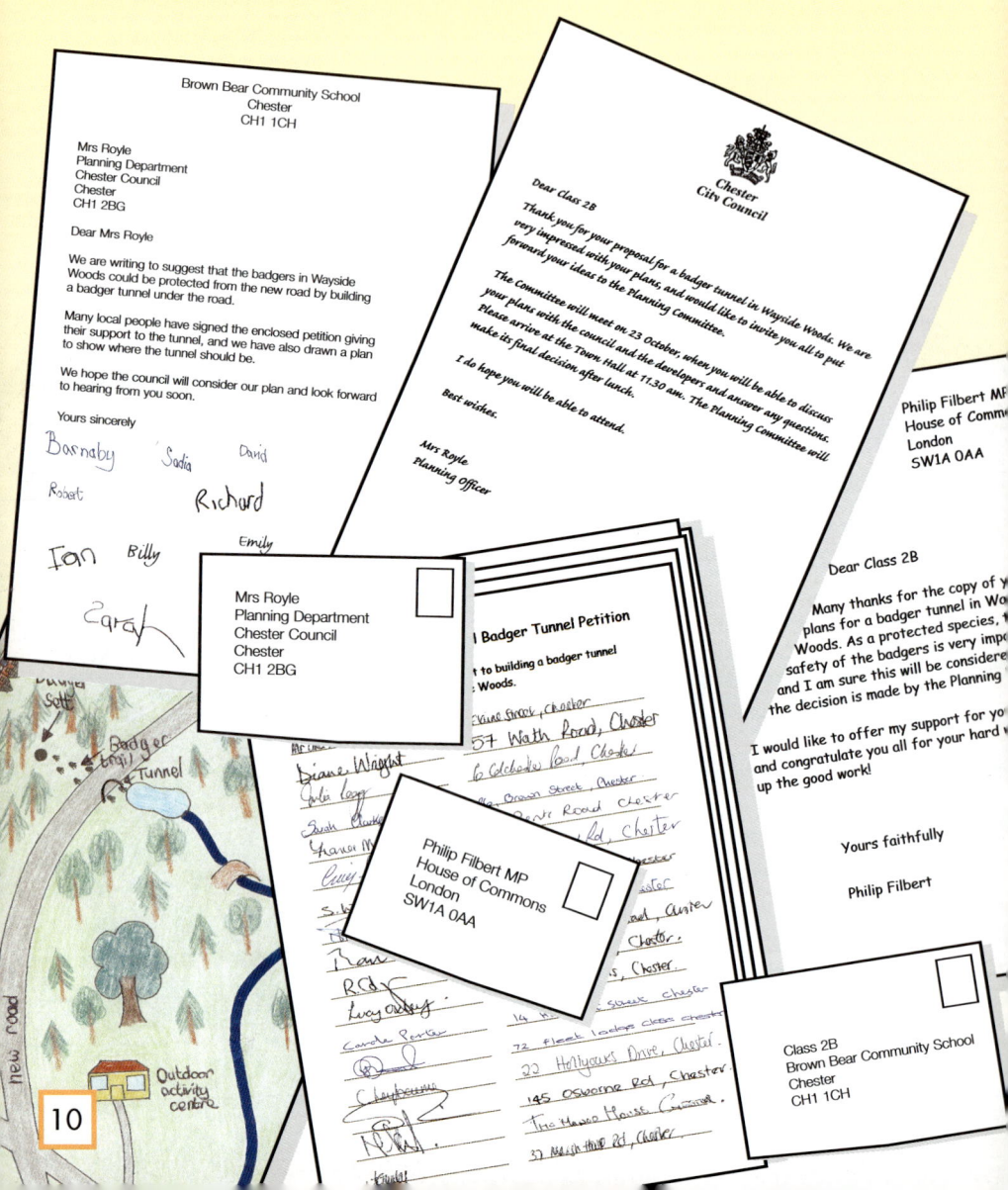

The Council agreed it would be worth the cost.
Without it the badgers could all have been lost.

When the tunnel was opened, the children felt good. They had saved all the badgers in Wayside Wood.